DEDICATION

Strength, clarity, honesty and authenticity
wrapped up in vulnerability, inner reflection and self truth.
Now shining with the stars.
You are loved.

MY PERSONAL GREAT THANKS TO:

My husband Mark, who simply sat in ceremony and waiting patiently for me to join him, I love you deeply.

Pitt, my first Shaman whose finesse in ceremony, great care and skill inspired me to welcome this world of plant medicine, ceremony and ritual deep into my being.

Pauli, my ceremonial wife - for our deep connection, her wisdom, love and devotion to the work.

Nicole, for smiling so widely in my kitchen as I asked if she would join me as Medicine Woman in a woman's circle with Madre, it turned out to be the start of this.

Fiona, my spirit sister - for her groundedness, her belief in me, her beauty and presence.

Murphy, my sister, for every single ounce of help and support and for turning up exactly at the right time to support me, without question and just because.

Livvie, my youngest daughter - for her laughter, joy, sense of adventure and for all the blessings she brought so intuitively to our ceremonies.

Rosi, my eldest daughter - for inspiring me, for your strength of character and for teaching me how to be more vulnerable and brave, just like you.

Without you all, this book would not have been written.

FOREWORD

This work is more than beautiful, it's more than powerful, it's more than soulful, it's more than inspiring. It just IS and it grabs you with the force of a hurricane and the gentleness of a soft summer breeze.

As I was reading through this book, I became overwhelmed with the desire to hold its physical entity in my hands. I wanted to feel its weight and flick its pages. I also wanted to look at it the way one looks at a Bible, without opening it, just 'absorbing' it.

I love the way the sacred feminine shares its space with the sacred masculine.
That's quite a feat, and a rare 'vibration'.

I found my "blind angel" in these pages. I know her well.

I hope this book will crash through the relentless white noise that our society produces and reach the souls who are silently crying for it.

Gabrielle Blackman Sheppard
Mother, Grandmother, Wise Elder & Mental Health Advocate

THESE WORDS

May these words resonate through your very being and hold you in comfort on a lonely night.

May these words confirm your joy when you're in flow.

May these words remind you that your inner wisdom is all you need and is already within.

May these words bring women together in circle.

May these words open your ceremonies, rituals, gatherings, fire dances and moon-lit circles.

May these words start heartfelt conversations that connect women; nurture us and bring us together in love.

A'ho

BE GUIDED

Hold this book close to your heart.
Whisper, "What do I need?"
Where you open her will be your guided message.

Inspire your women's circle discussions.
Whisper, "What needs to be brought out in the open"
Where you open her will be a starting point for sharing circles.

Be blessed.

OPENING CEREMONY PRAYER

To the women who held us our whole lives, we give great thanks.

To the women around us who dance with us, sing with us, feel for us and impart their love and wisdom to us on a daily basis; we give great thanks.

To the wise women of our futures, the ones who aren't yet born, the ones who are still so young but will teach us the most - and to our sisters in this circle, we give great thanks.

This circle is now open.

A'ho

PERSONAL SELF GRATITUDE PRAYER

To the girl I used to be, I thank you.

To the woman I am now, you are exactly where you need to be.

To the woman I am yet to become, I see you.

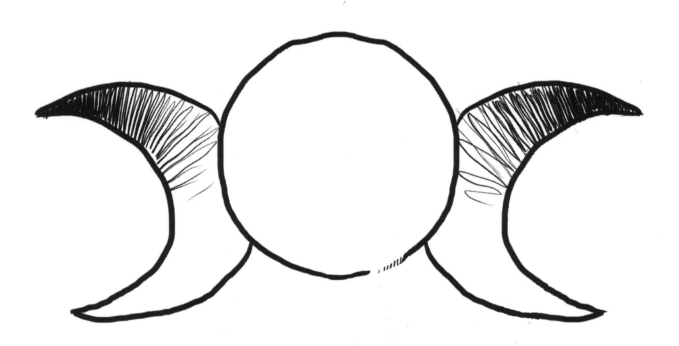

1

Ritual unearthed the sage in her,

Her devotion connecting the feminine.

Sisterhood, plant medicine, healing, creating, trusting her divine

In preparation for the feminine's collective rise;

Restoring women to ritual.

To unveil her power; securing her own space.

Deliberate thought, intention, guidance from universal sources.

Intuition blooming, sisters sat together in circle.

The masculine preparing to receive her strength, her fullness, her power.

Holding space with just a breath - he is ready to surrender for unity.

2

And then she realised
And smiled.
It was all in her hands.
The whole goddamn thing.

3

A priestess in renewal
Talking to the trees, they overheard her cries.
Sanctuary for her soul;
Protecting, accepting, holding sacred space.

A priestess in renewal;
Messy, lost, power.
They took her in, allowing courage, brilliance to glimmer.
Pachamama felt her, licked her tears,

Encouraged breath.
Distracted with beauty,
Held her thoughts,
The breadth of their span.

Father sky above, nature's recalibrator,
Infinity great and small.
Her ground, every thing
Stabilising, strong, source.

Vital energy for recognition.
Clouds clearing within -
Oxygen, spirit, support.
Everything she needed, right within her touch.

Magic, beauty, sisterhood, hers to let in
Expression, wildness, hurt to relief.
Her own crowning glory, giver of her own breath.
A priestess in renewal.

Wisdom released; grace invited to birth on fertile ground.
Flow, focus and intention
Breaking through with strength, stable once more and very, very clear.
A priestess renewed.

4

As she lay there in the darkness
Deeper in fear with every breath,
Her thoughts her worst energy,
Creating fiction, comparison, lack.

Vulnerability, sensitivity, ignition for imagination -
Then she remembered the now,
The only thing she really had
And she breathed in.

The smell of her covers, her pillow, her skin.
The touch of her curves, the stretch of her body,
The warmth of the safety she provides her self.
The comfort, protection, assurity in now.

She'd come this far; every single day,
Affirmations, trust, communion with self.
Breath, surrender, gifting control back to source.
Energy, frequency, her most valued offering, to soothe her Self back to calm.

5

That was the day she lost something.
The will to cover up, maintain the lie,
Smile to please, stroke ego to pacify.

Instead, she turned to truth and authenticity on a different level.
She'd rather have a relationship with no one
Than play out a conditional 'love' seeped with control.

She decided.
She took her life back.
It was she who approved of herself.

6

She was bored of it herself,
The topic that was.
She'd churned it around, upside down, inside out for so long
It was old.

And the churning of it kept it alive - in her frequency, whatever her words of letting go spoke.
So she left it alone, as best she could;
Let time take its distance,
Turn her passion to something else.

Let the universe work it out; allow vibration and energy to be her guide,
Having complete faith that everything would work out, and it would
Because her true self, her inner being, deepest guide, higher knowing needed nothing more
Than for her to find relief, pleasure and flow in every moment she breathed.

7

When one look said it all
And she opened her arms for her sister,
For tears to fall on her shoulder
That silence was the most precious thing in the world.

When everything else was complicated
She was the one who remained still.
Still by her side, unquestionable truth.
She had the ability to make everything ok.

8

She felt blessed to know she could soothe herself.

She felt blessed to understand how to make herself happy.

Most of all, she felt blessed enough to rely on her intuition.

9

She stood in her power.

Encouraged to say no

She grew up owning her body

And protecting her space.

She knew what she wanted,

Directed her time as she wished -

No limits, constraints or rules.

Just free.

Her third eye opened

Filled with joy, in flow

She sang and she danced, completely unaware

Of the adults who noticed and commented and smiled,

Wishing they'd known the same, been given their power.

And in their noticing of a powerful girl, they grew their own wings

And flew, just like her; with her often, even when she had disappeared right out of sight.

10

To her ancestors, she bowed her head.

To her future lineage - in spirit, on earth and in dreams, she kissed her fingertips.

To women alive right now in her time, she touched the earth for them.

Never ever in the history of the world had the feminine been so secure in its rising.

11

The pleasure was all hers.

Every inch, every move

Inviting her own body, responding to her own need.

An ache, a sacred honour - pleasure her birthright

By herself, for herself, knowing herself

In admiration, heady awe for her beauty, her power, her body.

Intoxicating, self pleasure, lightness of touch

Bringing her closer, back arching, a parting for the heat of the sun to find her.

Breath slow, deliberate swiftness spinning her, whipping her up into delight,

Beautiful, intoxicating, a delicate balance of thrill, delight, firmness and depth.

Delicious tumbling and rising, intensifying

Reaching fever pitch, rolling round, tipping her over

Until finally falling pushing her, finding her, thrilling her, wetting her through delight.

Every inch, every move, the pleasure was all hers.

12

She'd seen her break and lose her ground, fall apart.
She'd seen her in the depths of confusion and utter disbelief.
She'd met her in deep shame, held her hand in "Why?"
She saw her, she knew her, she loved her anyway.

For to hold space for a sister,
For her to fall apart in despair
Yet have her reputation maintained, honoured and recited back to her
Is to provide sanctuary - a heaven on earth.

Because falling apart is not 'her',
It's simply a space in time to feel at her deepest level
And to be held as sacred, special and seen.
Is both her right and yours too.

13

And then she realised

That pain was familiar.

She'd been here before,

An emptiness in the pit of her being.

A void, a hole, a longing.

But this time was different,

She was whole now.

A different person;

Time travelling herself,

Feeling her way, eyes closed, in a dark room and completely secure.

This time she couldn't crumble.

The universe had broken her, to rebuild her with earth,

She was made of pachamama now and she touched her every day.

14

Why?
Because she could,
Because she had capacity.
Because she was strong.
Because she was a mother.

15

And she said to herself

"You did so very well, you saved yourself, and I noticed",

And she had done well.

As she sat and contemplated

Her shoulders relaxed, she breathed deeply.

She closed her eyes and smiled for herself,

She had finally remembered who she was.

She saved herself and she knew it.

She did it every time

She honoured her rite of passage.

She nourished herself,

She took pleasure in her self,

She forgave herself.

She stayed close to her feminine tribe and honoured the divine in her and them.

16

She felt every step,

Listening through the noise.

Intentions close, hearing silent whispers.

Hand on her heart, embracing self growth,

Trusting, closing tear filled eyes.

Nurturing inner child

Aware that every move

Leads her to something new.

Blind angel, she can't see so she feels her way instead;

Gathering her wildness,

Those who could see for her, showered her with love.

Chaotic vulnerability in the middle of it all

While carefree relief vibrated just below.

She had ground, oxygen and spirit.

Blissful revealing, re-connection and favour,

She was seen. She was seen. She was seen.

17

For her daughters...
She expected them to fall and wonder how they're going to get back up,
She expected them to hurt and wonder how it happened,
She expected them to fall in love and get taken over by someone else's passion and wonder how they lost themselves.
She expected that they will be run ragged and then question how to find themselves in the chaos,
She expected them to experience times of deep joy and revel in how incredible their life is,
She expected them to stumble over solitude and wonder how to navigate their way through loneliness.
She expected them to crash into disappointment, to break and to question their purpose in life.

And for her...
She expected to fall and then show them how she got back up,
She expected to talk about how she got hurt and how she took responsibility for her own heartbreak.
She expected to one day explain how she fell in love and lost herself in someone else, finding her deepest souls work because of it.
She expected to show them how, when she was run ragged, she recovered herself with privacy, meditation, writing, plant medicine and sacred sisterhood.
She expected to share how she revelled in the joys of being alive, being inspired, being in love with herself.
She expected to talk deeply and meaningfully about when she felt loss and loneliness and how she navigated her way through the pain.
She expected herself to be brave enough to shine a light on her own disappointments and talk about how 'breaking' is another word for 'renewal' and 'fresh' starts.

And then...

She expected them to ignore it all and find their own beautiful path.

She expected their path to be different, and their life purpose to be expressly and uniquely theirs.

She expected to learn from them,

She looked forward to listening when they asked her to,

She looked forward to them being unavailable to her because they were distracted by their own life quests.

And she LOVED, LOVED, LOVED that they were free to explore their world through their own eyes

And she loved knowing that their connection would remain energetically and very tangibly to both their highest good.

18

Her morning ritual was her strength,
Gone was the belief that another could nourish her soul.
Precious time to create practices for herself opened up
Grounding, breathing and ritual
Nourished her spirit,
Her super power, her connection to source
And she was bringing her Self home.

19

The joy of being able to hear
Her quietened mind so still, barely sensing breath.
She was home, back to source,
Connecting to the goddess within
Her Self, higher power, her guiding light.

Magic worked there -
In silence, being guided,
Detachment, focus, an art.
She heard her through the silence,

Barely a breath whispered,
Serenity washed over
Taking her deeper with each rise.
Tranquil immersion at its finest, truest, deepest clarity

And she never wanted to leave.
Soaking up extra precious seconds as she felt her rise
Falling back, awareness engaged
And into the dream she awoke.

20

She asked, she pleaded, made vision boards, called angels
And she couldn't hear a damn thing, nothing changed and everything failed.
She got pummelled and pushed and crushed and melted
And swallowed up whole by the tide.

So she threw it all in the air
Walked away, said "F**k you!"
Stopped everything, focused on surviving
Hour by hour, day by day, breathing, functioning, staying alive

And for months she struggled -
Upside down, no ground,
Being swept along with the wind,
Clawing for grip.

And then one day, she looked up at the sky,
Clear, no clouds, a breeze, relief
And joy and love and faith with such hold.
Unimaginable strength, glorious, naked worship.

Her work had been done,
from deep within
her Self forged a path and she started to walk.
She asked and relaxed, envisioned and whispered,

Standing in the wind like someone who owned her world.
Angels stood with her,
Planets moved out of her way
Revealing her runway, her flow and her time.

21

She woke up one morning
In the wrong life,
With no damn idea.
Shock ruptured her soul,

Searching for something -
Nothing was there.
Shaken to her core,
Anxiety fuelled sad

Tears stung her face,
Panic ripped her heart,
Sadness stole her eyes
And truth ran through cold.

She woke up one morning
"You got yourself in this, you get yourself out!"
She focused in tight
On glimpses of light,

One day at a time
She got out of her hole.
Freedom felt close,
Energy soared.

A decision was made,
She trusted herself,
Walked straight out the door
And let her wings bring her home.

22

She hadn't expected to feel that.
As tears rolled down her face
It dawned on her, that feeling.
The murkiness inside.
She took it from the shadows,
How did shame get right in there?
In that place she'd kept so strong
And clear and focused with her quiet.

Then it dawned on her.
She remembered, in her moment of vulnerability
She'd taken someone way too close
And let them straight inside.
Insidious silent tones disguised as love
Had swept her off her feet,
Drenched her in a pool of doubt,
Of fear and sadness she'd hidden.

Her laughter brought her back to now,
She saw it as it was!
Her head thrown back, she laughed out loud,
"It's gone!" Her heart was clear.
The clouds just disappeared for her,
Relief and calm swept through.
She reinstated love and breathed,
"You're back, my love, you're back!"

She thanked her lucky stars, the moon, her source and love itself.
A tremor might have thrown her
But connection brought her back.
With trust, intention and ritual
She had melted shame away.
A stronger, wiser queen emerged,
Nourished, honoured, healed and whole.

23

Her connection with Patience started the moment she blasted

"I'm f***ing coming!"

Mother to daughter, messy, flares flew.

Disconnect, a breakage, wounds and shame exposed.

Grief and tears poured out of her -

How had it got to that?

Too much is how it got to that.

Too many demands, too many requests, too much 'all' for anyone, too much.

Sinking into deep wounds, ashamed to call herself,

Just a little girl caught up in myths of what it meant to shine.

To shine is to glow, to glow is to feel, to feel is to feel EVERY THING.

To revel in her humanness she came here to expand.

Deep breaths were her friend, stopping streams of requests identifying - just one.

Pausing to listen more, clarifying what was most important,

With a little one turning, tumbling emotions,

Fire in her heart, fierce independence brewing and a mother reclaiming her Self.

One day at a time, one request at a time, explaining more, slowing down,

Her season changed, vibrations levelled, she felt her ground with each new stage.

The meltdowns, the drama's, the reasoning with the unreasonable - with

Opportunities for smoother paths.

Sitting with stillness in unpredictable tornados,

Breathing through storms so wild she thought she might break.

Maintaining her state, leading with cool,

She smoothed, she slowed, she smiled.

For every single slow motion breath

Rising and falling to the rhythm of her heart;

Wisdom, stardust, she smiled within.

Patience had met her there.

24

Wild feminine healing force
Surrendering to the sand,
Throwing magic in the air.
Ritual, trusting universal law,

Her power to create
Rising, powerful, healing force,
Intention and inspiration
A potent feminine brew.

Bravery forged
An expression of her wildness,
All to show the divine feminine future
Her very own sparkly, glittery flame.

25

She lit up the room, even in darkness
Her presence felt, serene and still,
Alert to every single sound.
Tiptoeing barefoot through layered worlds,
Grace and stealth, deliberate steps,
Intention, steady and strong.

Their queen of the throne,
Their hand, their blessing.
No words, just a pillar of support.
The queen of ceremony,
Energy flowing through
Then closing ritual with laughter and fun.

Hugs and chatter, relief and so much love
Sparkling like fresh dew in the breaking morning light.
Energy cleansed, lessons learned.
Sisterhood, resurrection, fertile ground,
Gratitude to the plants, the sacred, the Shaman,
The power of the feminine - Shamama.

26

It bewildered her really,
How magically everything appeared
Right in front of her, to touch and hold
Once she let go of the illusion of reality.

27

She had no choice but to let go.

Her thoughts a delicious mix of turmoil, fire, passion.

Exhausting, threatening, manifesting

And she saw her power right there.

Manifesting, crazy sh*t
Unfolding before her.
Betrayal, mistrust, soft words behind backs,
Too much, not enough, way too much.

Her land wasn't the same anymore,
And when she fell to her knees in those earthquakes,
Rubble crumbling under her feet,
She knew she was being buried alive

And she was crippled.
Crushed, heart ripped out,
Grief like she'd never known -
Broken, with a hole straight through her heart.

A third cup took her further than she'd ever been before;
To see so clearly why, the purpose, the reason,
The break. Right there, crystal clear.
Her heart had been broken, to be welded with gold -

Her soul's contract needing to be fulfilled.
The queen was being summoned
As she rose from the floor,
Clutching shells whispering, "Thank you, I love you, thank you."

She started afresh, brand new, reborn
And in time she grew, ushered by breath.
Took the reins, led her march
With power and softness and overflowing love for her Self.

28

She was the type of girl now who slipped off by herself
To commune with the trees and the ground and the sky.
To listen to birds, to hear spirits in the breeze.
To connect with her Self and steady the fizz.

She was the type of girl now who slipped off her boots
To soak up the earth, disperse energy, feel flow.
To listen to her breath, to hear more than could be said,
To connect with source and know all was love.

29

No-one could have told her
What lay ahead through fear -
The challenge of the fire, the storm,
What lay ahead through fear.

No-one could have told her
The relief, the trust, the peace -
She had absolutely no idea,
What lay ahead through fear.

No-one could have told her
Divine support, immaculate timing,
Presence felt, effortless peace.
That's what lay ahead through fear.

No-one could have told her
What her smile would feel like now.
Secure soul and stable flow,
That's what lay head through fear.

30

Sacred cacao… her spirit lit her creativity,
Bathed her soul in delight,
Soothed her senses with love,
Flooded her heart with contentment.
Connected, level and balanced,
She had never known beauty so deep.
To feel at home deep inside,
To trust with such force
That she couldn't fall, she was held.

31

"You shine too bright", she was told.

"Dim your light a little", she was told.

"Others are feeling a little uncomfortable", she was told.

"Your song is too much", she was told.

"A little boastful", she was told.

So she listened and thanked her and appreciated her thoughts

And shone brighter instead, stood her ground, felt so clear

Trusting in the divine,

Knowing deeply that another womans fire

Will not ignite in the shadow of her dimming hers.

32

Burn the candle,
Smoke the sage,
Whisper your blessings.
Breathe out your fears,
This moment is yours.

33

And she spent time talking to herself.

In fact, she was the very best person to talk to.

She got her,

She listened as she needed,

She allowed her Self to cry without fuss or commotion,

Just to let the tears drip and her breath calm.

She loved that time by herself.

She needed it.

The words on the page,

The words spoken out loud so she could hear them for herself.

The thoughts, the patterns, the aha's!

They were all a necessary part of her - her sanity, her peace, her balance

And so she continued to spend time with herself

In gratitude, in love and in perfect alignment.

She loved her Self so very much.

34

The more she awoke

The more she realised,

There are signs EVERYWHERE!

Tuned in, tapped in, she saw what was hidden before.

The more she listened

The more she learned,

Everyone was her guru.

Every single person had something of value for her.

Something to ingest, a word, a phrase, a look, a realisation, an emotion

And so she continued to tune in,

Closed her mouth more,

Listened with more intention,

Cleared her heart so love could flow in

And the more she did

The more she awoke.

35

She learned about her vibration.

She had glimpses of what it was like to vibrate clean and high and in love -

She'd felt it and even though sometimes it slipped through her fingers, she recognised its sensation

And she realised, by meeting lower vibrations at their level she simply activated more of that in her own life.

So she spent a little time and care

Centering herself, grounding her own activation, taking care of her own feelings

So she could meet any vibration and not get knocked off her feet by their wind and drama and chaos.

Her alignment was paramount, her stability fierce.

To grow in that fertile soil, creative energy, joyous power

Ooooooh… how she revelled in that wonder.

36

She released the need to hide the parts of herself she didn't like
With candle, with intention, with thought.
She had had enough of feeling less, not enough, a little broken.
She gathered those parts of her from the shadows,
Brought them out into the open,
Loved them, saw their fragility, spoke so softly to them
And asked them to shine,
Gave them permission to be seen, to join the beauty in her
And held their hand as they rose up to meet her.
She was one, she was whole, she was love.

37

She was not intimidating, they were intimidated.

She was not broken, she was healing.

She was not sad, she was feeling.

She was not losing, she was gaining.

Those are the words she wished she'd heard back then,

But she told herself now, every single damn day

And her heart grew.

38

She had no fear this time,

She just decided

And that, right there, was a contract bound with herself, sealed with love.

Authentic, prepared to stand alone, to honour herself,

Forge her path, she knew what to do next.

She trusted and loved that, for some, she was reckless,

For others, she was brave.

For her, it was a sure thing

And that was all that mattered.

39

The world needed her softness, her sacredness, her depth.

The world needed her wisdom, strength & intuition.

The world needed to feel her ancient heart power, her flow and her life force,

But she needed to remember it first.

40

Let them walk away,

Release yourself from their grip,

Loosen their hold,

Protect your most precious gift.

Give power to your sacredness - not theirs.

Offer symbolism to the universe to tap into your higher power.

Speak your words of release like spells,

Use your charms like magic,

Weave your inner circle with finesse.

Reveal your true strength,

For you can do anything you put your mind to.

History has no bearing on your future now,

The book is not written.

Each step, another word, it's safe,

So safe. Let them go and commune with the rivers of power running through your spine instead.

You are love, you are loved, you are safe*

[* WITH VERY KIND PERMISSION TO USE - THESE WORDS ARE FROM MY DEAR SOUL SISTER
CHLOE BRADBURY RUTHERFORD]

41

Over those years she had unlearnt movement,
The courage to express with her body, dimmed.
Shyness, stiffness, she'd rather watch and sit out,
But something inside her told her -
Move! Dance! Express!
She knew she would rise, move, remember who she was if she let inhibition go.

Private moments revealed old moves… still there… just beneath.
Music prompted solo exploration,
Reclaiming her body,
Placing herself in unknown territory.
Feeling the pain of a timid heart and a brave soul reaching,
Reclaiming her power, such relief.

42

She is a brave, beautiful woman.
She will one day do something with such grace,
Something that from where she stands now, would seem so completely ridiculous!
But she will do it, and she will do it like it's the next easy step, a walk in the park, no big deal.

43

One day she will look back on her younger self,

Fly through time to be with her,

Place a hand on her heart and breathe with her,

Allowing all of her gratitude to flow into her.

That young woman who struggled so much

Will have no idea she is being thanked,

That her work, courage and bravery is being honoured,

Or that her future is holding the bravest, purest, sexiest version of herself she could ever imagine.

44

It wasn't just for her that the feminine had to rise, it was for him too,

For when the masculine holds space for the feminine, the feminine frees the masculine.

When She is held in high esteem by a brother who sees HER,

When She is held by his presence and breath,

She can breathe and create freely, conjuring spirit and colour and sense into realms way beyond his knowing alone.

When he stands by her side as author, creator, poet, teacher and shaman, the world expands.

When our brothers feel our strength and weave it delicately with theirs,

When our brothers trust our senses and seek our wisdom where they can not see,

When our shadows become one and we melt into the purest forms of each other,

Our worlds co-create and our visions of what the world COULD look like

Shake and shift and shape and reform and heal and soothe;

Together they will lead and heal and nurture and calm.

She is here, she is breathing and walking towards him from the shadows.

He is preparing, calling her in, making space, releasing resistance.

He is holding her hand in solidarity.

45

With fairy lights and journals and pens and soft blankets,

With candles and cushions with throws and cacao,

With indulgence and focus and spirit and intention,

With alone time, with daughters, with best friends, with self -

Just be there, revel there, write it out, put words on pages.

For healing, for smoothing your path, for blessing, for ritual,

For deep care and for strength and for the filling up of creativity,

For swirling around in love, just for the sake of it, the bliss and the soul.

Just be there, for you, create heaven.

46

Because she was young,
Because she knew as much as she knew,
Because she had been let down,
Because she had been so desperately hurt,
Because she had never known trust,
She sent her love.
Peace, blessings, forgiveness, it's ok.
Not despite her hurt,
But because of it.

47

Hold her, put everything else down.

Make it sacred, special, divine.

She's so little, even with her long hair and her big words and her fierce strength,

She is little, she needs you, your smell, your touch, her safety.

You're her mother, you're her everything, her ground, her sky, her heart.

Connect deeply.

'Feel' her mood, ask her, seek her opinion.

Your words are spells that will capture her heart and be etched in her memory.

Your words will sink deep into her spirit, and help her nurture herself as she grows.

And she will grow, she will blossom, eventually she will let go

And she will be brave and courageous and smart and self sufficient.

Self sufficient enough to be her own sanctuary, her own divine.

To know solidly who she is, to regard herself as sacred, wondrous, striking -

And she will never quite know how she knows herself, with such purity, where that knowledge came from,

It will just be.

Deeply seated in her body, absorbed forever in her heart

She will move around the world with assurity, love and security,

Because she was made from love, intention, flow, laughter and she was cherished every single step.

48

Bliss is waking up first,
Breathing in the freshness of a new morning,
Lingering over the aroma of Cacao,
Closing your eyes and tuning into your Self.

49

She had to live, to feel and to experience.

To die, to survive, to drown and then draw breath,

Because somewhere there was another woman,

Struggling, lost and confused

And she knew that one day her words would land on her heart so damn hard,

That she will remember her life has meaning and substance again.

Her words, her strength will help another draw breath and stay alive,

Just like she did.

50

"Isn't it strange?" She pondered,
How somewhere in the world, there was a woman.
She didn't know her name,
But their paths were destined to cross
And she would come to mean the world to her.

51

It was hard to let go of the feeling of 'not enough',

So highly tuned to comparison to another woman -

Thighs, skin, smile, hair, age,

Yet absolutely none of it made the slightest difference to the light she carried in her soul.

52

She knew so deeply in her body

That letting her old self disappear

Was the only way to grow into the woman she was about to become;

But still she mourned her passing.

53

She created her altar

One rock at a time,

Not quite sure of what she was doing,

But doing what felt right.

Listening to stones,

Whispering to leaves,

Breathing in flowers -

Reminders of precious people.

A space to fill her heart

Just for her, where no-one else went.

Privacy, dedicated time,

Intention for celebration, healing, tears, finding her Self.

She started, holding space for herself

And she loved every single damn second.

54

She had only been through that pain because she was strong enough to hold it.

55

She was following her heart and her heart alone,
Taking the time to sense every movement.
Ritual was confirming,
Meditation her guide.
Stopping when she wobbled,
Walking away when her human mind questioned -
Nothing about this made any sense,
Yet with her hand on her heart, she beamed,
She bravely acted
Without expectation to articulate,
Just knowing this was her path.

56

Each and every woman walked into that space

With beauty in their soul

Calm, called to be there, prepared for Madre

The goddess in them stepping forward

The warrior determined to emerge

Wanting this, being called back to their essence

Space filled with incense, white, feminine

Candles lit, space held, breath felt

Stillness radiating, ready to dive deep

Their stories heard, shared wounds loosening their grip

Strangers turned sisters, feeling energy

Love radiating in that circle

Intuition stirring

Senses alight

They merged that night, stirring centuries of healing, trauma, guilt, shame, abuse

And transforming it into light, healing, love, power

Oh those women, sisters glowing,

Waking, so quiet, respect for self and fellow queens.

There is nothing like this, anywhere, ever.

The bond, the strength, the unspoken power and adoration

Of women in circle.

A blessing, their blessing

Paving way for future women, the little girls of now

To explore themselves untethered, unfettered, unashamed

To walk in their glow.

Women past -

They paved the way for us,

Now we forge way for them.

Such bliss,

So blessed,

A woman's blessing.

A'ho.

57

She stopped worrying, allowed everything to move at its own pace.

Relinquished stress, permitted herself to be a beginner.

Surrendered control in return for flow,

Recognised source as the home of happiness.

Made peace with her past,

Believed in miracles,

Trusted intuition,

Thanked her self for guiding her through.

Focused only on her journey,

Revealing in her growth, maturity, glow.

It all made sense when she stopped,

Allowing everything to move at its own pace.

58

SPACE

The gap between reflection and deflection of the self.

Sacred; private; alone,

For expression, writing, tears, joy, pleasure, pain, honouring, ritual, intention.

Intuitively led: 'to make space for her Self'.

59

And she hummed to begin with, so discreet, hoping no-one would know,

Hidden by the chords, the volume, the circle.

Eyes closed, in her own world, she breathed out her tune,

Song filling her head, her volume rose, voice cracking with fear.

It was her heart, so full she could barely contain it,

Energy rising, voice forming song, courage filling up,

Raising vibration, trusting the words, harmony, tune, those notes filling the air.

In flow with her soul, finding strength in the dark, sinking so deep in the medicine,

Blossoming from heart.

It was hers, feminine sacredness, goddess rising within her, filling her space.

Permission granted, but not only that; her voice had to be heard

For healing, for trust, for journeying, for depth.

Her gift to the collective, her hand on her heart,

To grant permission for every woman.

Energetic tuning, her sister, HER song.

For her voice heals too, her voice must be trusted,

Her words, her whispers, her volume,

She is given smooth passage.

She hummed, spoke and sang. Whispering deep into the night...

She told her sisters, it's time.

60

As she watched her move through the crowd, she thought
What made her beautiful, was not her shape or her hair or her skin,
But the swagger when she moved,
The slowness in which she stepped,
The can't care, won't care of her mood.
The way she ate, thoughtful and appreciative,
The depth in her eyes when she caught your stare.
Her power,
Her audacity,
Her laugh.
She was the most beautiful woman there.

61

Tiredness washed over her.

Brain running like an engine,

Whirring, noisy, chaotic

Heart beating fast.

Anxiety. Panic. Overwhelm.

So she found herself some sunlight and sat right in it,

Breathed, slow breaths, her thudding heart in her chest.

For a long time she was there, everything waited.

She felt the warmth, some calm, some slow,

A blanket soothed her skin,

A pillow carried her mind,

And she rested, and breathed and slept.

A whisper brought her back, "You were right."

62

They called her a strong woman, powerful, a queen even, but she knew
Sometimes it was a compliment, sometimes… well… not.
But she was strong because she had learnt,
She had learned because she'd been burnt,
She had been burnt because she'd said yes
And she had said yes, because she was brave.

63

When she said yes to another, it seemed to mean no for her.
She missed out, kept giving, it was the right thing to do.
'Being kind is important', she thought
And she wanted to help, had been taught to help

And others liked her for her help,
And they asked for more -
Which was given with love,
Then more and some more and some more.

Without realising it, one day she sank.
Nothing left, she broke. Exhausted, crashed, crumpled, too much.
And so it took time. A long time.
To heal, to mend, to rest

And when she had energy, the real work started.
"Yes" became "I will if I can."
"Yes" became "Let me think about it."
She relearnt her language, her language of love.

64

Self nurture was her ritual,

Her own wishes worshipped,

Her most fantasized dreams imagined.

Boundaries protected,

Respecting and protecting those of her sisters in return.

That's how she became an empress.

65

With a wry smile she decided;

Every woman needs a story she can barely tell for laughing.

Every woman needs a story that wells her up so much, she has to wave her hand in front of her face

to get through it.

Every woman needs a story of unrequited love,

Every woman needs a story that shocks her sons and daughters,

As they learn about each other as adults.

Every woman needs a story of bravery, of courage, of extreme daring,

Every woman needs a story of a love that lasted a lifetime

And every woman needs a secret that she will never divulge to anyone.

66

And she realised that being nice, sometimes made her look subservient,

That in being nice, she gave way to what she preferred,

In being nice, she put her own needs second.

In being nice, others walked in their paths and trampled all over hers.

And so one day

It came from nowhere,

A consequence, a decision, a stake in the ground.

A damn huge wall of fire and energy, with eyes clear and a voice that enforced;

"Me first", "I'm important", "I'm honouring this boundary" and "This is where it ends."

And with deep breaths, the clearest of vision

And the best choice of words she could conjure up,

She was kind, but she said no.

She was nice, but she stated her preferences.

She was gentle, but her boundaries were strong.

Relieved, elated, worthy, energetic and liberated

She knew she'd broken an ancestral chain of compliancy, bitterness, regret & pain,

Exonerating generations of women before her.

She was free. And so were her daughters.

67

What she needed most, more than anything in the world, was rest,

Deep, nurturing, guilt free, blessed rest.

To stop. To sleep.

To be fed nourishing food that tasted sublime, that stimulated every cell to recover.

She needed restorative, soul nutrition.

Somewhere to be, without question, without needing to answer.

No pressure to speak even, to compare, to 'do'.

Somewhere to hide just for a bit.

Somewhere safe in the company of trusted sisters who understood the need for seclusion,

A retreat,

A womb to be held in,

Just for a while.

For this strong powerful warrior was out of everything, depleted, sore and tired

And she knew if she took her time,

Listened to her soul,

She would grow beyond any version of herself she could ever create in her mind…

She was listening. The time had come.

68

When she remembered why she was here
It all made sense,
In that moment, she wiped her eyes.
Relief washed through her body
And she felt her ground again,
She knew she was ok.

69

Her higher self smiled,

"That's it, you're doing it, keep going!"

She noticed synchronicity, played with opportunity, danced with coincidence.

Everything flowed, felt easy, fell into place, started to move,

Conversations were happening, smiles exchanged, friends connecting.

"I have your back", she heard.

"Learn and grow", she was told.

"I'm with you."

It was the most powerful message she had ever received.

70

The wind howled around her,

The planets shifted above her,

Father Sky darkened and threw his forces at her so hard it winded her.

The ground broke beneath her,

But she held her own.

Euphoric, vulnerable, crown in place, steady, unfuckablewith,

Her inner goddess flamed, a sensual bliss owned.

Fear, guilt, shame transmuted to pleasure and power, her birthright.

Unfettered magic, liberty, fertility, sacred flow.

Source rising, inner stillness and peace.

Pure, abundance, free flowing peace

Ran through her like a cool river on a summer's day

And she bathed in the sunlight of sisterhood.

71

And she breathed,

And she breathed,

And she breathed,

And she breathed,

And she breathed.

72

She woke up one day and realised after all of that,
She was in fact, still breathing.
After everything she had done, lived through, tried, experienced,
She was still breathing
And so she started to trust in her breath.

Breath became her friend, her stability, her inner sanctuary,
No matter what storm, hurricane or howling wind pushed her,
Her own breath kept her steady. And when she felt steady,
She could walk anywhere.

73

She felt her pain so deeply,
A little girl wanting her fathers love.
Attention, asking, eyes firmly on him
And he kept her waiting,
Eventually, she turned her head away.

74

A circle of women

Holding space,

A rite of passage

To hold with breath without judgement, comparison, jealousy.

It takes awareness, a love of self and a connection to a higher source

To understand that her decision, is your decision,

Her choice, is your choice,

Her way is yours, given the same circumstances.

A circle of women

Holding space,

A rite of passage

To hold her with respect, with compassion, with love and protection.

To have her back,

To stand next to her as she fights to vibrate higher,

For her triumph, is yours too.

Her sacred flow, a running river of love, is yours to bathe in also.

75

The day she found her voice
Was the day she stood back from old patterns long enough
To recognise them for what they were.
Thin layers of parchment, shielding her from the beauty of growth,
That was when she let her through,
Her spirit, her sensuality, her taste, her touch,
Her higher self held her hand and whispered the way,
She trusted it with every fibre.

She changed a little,
Others couldn't quite recognise her.
She stopped resisting, found flow and acted purely on inspiration
And when she flew, others called her 'lucky', 'blessed', 'favoured',
But seeing through the eyes of source was her magic.
Retreating inside for stillness was her healing
And when her sacred feminine rose to meet her,
That was her gift.

76

She raised her daughter to say no, be defiant, stand her ground,
To ask for what she wanted, to appreciate her unfolding gifts,
To notice when she was in flow and how her emotions guided her.

She raised her daughter to know gentleness and kindness, ritual and gratitude,
To ask her intuition, to navigate her way, through thought and ceremony,
To notice when she needed quiet time, solitude, stimulation or excitement.

And he raised her right by her side, to feel both the feminine and masculine,
To resist societal conditioning, see straight through the tricks of control, like shame and silence,
To be fearless, stand in her own flooding spotlight,
Because she owned her own mighty power and nothing else would ever matter.

77

She finally learned - don't chase, be still, play your own game.

She finally learned that their silence is your answer,

That their closed door was her nudge back onto her own divine pathway.

A mirror held up to shock her that old patterns still re-emerge, are still live in her vibration,

That the pain of the crush is just ego, that alignment never hurts.

She focused in, on the whole of herself, aligning with ritual, source, pachamama,

Making ceremony to lay her younger fears to rest with love,

For she was never taught to own her own sphere, her own draw,

Never taught the power of her own magnetic power -

And boy that power was there. She felt it in every deep meditation,

Where separation occurred and the connection that was always present became her ONLY present.

She felt that pull. Magnificent, strong, magnetic, floating her gently across a vibrational sea,

Always there. She taught her Self

Through the chaos, because in a windstorm, she realised there was no other cover but inside herself.

78

Ancient voices, pouring cooled water over her confused forehead,

Whispering secrets of synchronicity, melting human rationality, seriousness and fear.

"It's just a game", she heard. "Look for beauty", they said.

Uncoiling her heart, unchaining her beliefs, rewiring neural pathways to remember childhood knowing -

This was her message for every woman.

Answers are not where problems lie, they come when focus falls on silent sands.

She put herself in water, deep baths, showers pouring over her, washing her clean to start afresh,

She took herself off for silence, just a few minutes, feeling the sun on her face,

Allowing warmth to glow on her skin.

Intentional space was what she created, outside of chaos, motherhood, subscribed expectations,

Consciously allowing her senses to emerge through the turmoil of life.

Nothing more. Just intentional space.

Placing her hand on her heart, feeling turmoil, space to settle,

Sensing muddled, confused, dizzy vibrations falling away, just intentional space,

Her message for every woman.

79

When the sun shone through the cracks, she learned to bask in its glow.

80

She was everything.

The sun-blessed nurturer that kissed hurts better,

The butterfly that flitted here, there and everywhere,

The furious wind that blew a storm up and expressed her anger in the moment,

The coolest ocean waters that soothed volcanos and knew exactly what to do.

The still perfect petal, elevated on a passing breeze with nothing to do but bask in her own beauty

And a sacred goddess, revered for her grace and elegance, inspiration and strength.

A sister, a mother, a child, a lover, a daughter, a fairy, a spirit,

She was everything.

81

She strode right into the roaring seas until her thighs were drenched with wash.
Unsteady on her feet, trusting the movement, becoming one with turmoil,
Diving head first into the froth, mermaid disappearing into crashing waves,
To re-emerge the sylph with the pearl that everyone else only wished they'd found.

82

She learned to expect her transformation to be messy, turbulent, seemingly lawless.

There were times when she sobbed, fighting for breath and praying

For gravity to connect her to the earth.

Yet even in those moments, she felt everything coming together for her highest good.

Even in those moments, she felt held by a thousand women behind her,

Ancestors, spirits, witches, croans, children, all whispering goodness,

Filling her with spirit,

For she was forging the way ahead for her grandchildren.

83

She never consciously tried to heal him,

His wounds were deep, only she saw the scars that he masked for others with humour.

She felt blessed to be shown his authenticity.

When he asked her opinion she was flattered, assuming he valued her view.

Years later she realised it was because he doubted himself

And his self doubt ate away at them both.

She moulded herself to fit his trauma -

Did more, took the pressure off, took control.

She had capacity, energy, nerve and willingness

And above all, she had love to pour over broken wings and stinging scars.

She hushed and caressed and counselled and loved,

Until she had nothing left.

And it happened so fast. Nothing. No energy, no zest, no life.

Her fire just an ember, she had consumed herself, put her own flame out and she never even realised

Her love couldn't heal his hurt and his broken wings couldn't fan her flame,

For she realised too late that her power had scarred him deeper.

Her energy had shone bright enough to blind his own judgement even further,

Her absence was the only thing that would save him and if she didn't leave, she too would die.

84

And sometimes tears just fell, tipped over an edge by something,

Unable to hold back a waterfall, drenching everything around her

And there was nothing to be done but accept and surrender.

'Trust' and 'Movement' too big for today,

So she did her best to nourish her soul,

To seek oxygen, to be kind, to not label any thing or mood or feeling,

Just to sink and to remember that dark needs light and light needs dark.

Moods will lift, tears will dry and movement will happen… it is law.

85

This time when she put her hands together and her lips reached her fingers she whispered

"I'm in",

and "I'm all yours",

For she realised the universe had a plan

And she wasn't privy to it.

Neither, she knew, did she need to be -

For what she asked for, was so far out of her comfort zone,

That if it came to her today, right here, right now, it would scare the living daylights out of her.

She knew that each day she could only ask for as much as she could handle, digest, take in, appreciate.

What she really needed to do was relax, let it go, busy herself with playful things that brought her joy

And leave the mechanics, the magic, careful organising and skilful coincidences

To the energy that created worlds.

Surrender was her promise.

Devotion to pleasure her intention.

86

It melted her heart, rushing through her lungs like a wash of fresh, pure oxygen when she realised,

She was not being called to stand for anything dramatic - to fight or to win something hard,

She was just being called to let go.

For when she let go, she rose into the energy of her feminine,

Her authentic Self,

The real her,

And that by letting go and being more HER

She was nurturing the rise of the collective feminine.

Right here, right now by standing in the middle of her own bright flame.

87

And he never really knew how much his presence grounded her.

88

She gave up trying to prove her worth,

She knew it felt like sitting in a bath of anxiety and she was worth more than that.

So she just did her own thing,

Enjoyed her unfolding,

And blessed her gifts.

THE END

89

Even in her despair, she knew deeply

That her future would find her

And that the frustration of desperately trying to find 'it',

Like some metaphorical needle in a haystack

Exhausted her, consumed her and overtook her sanity.

It was the work of outdated programming.

The wise soul within soothed her enough.

The medicine woman unbound her eyes and untied her hands.

The pain dissipated,

Her physical body embraced surrender.

The energies of spirit, of Shamen past, as they blew tobacco in her face and purified her soul,

Clothed her like a second skin,

Assuring her that breath had cleansed her soul

And the strength of the Mother was close.

90

She learned to like the parts of her that felt broken.
She learned to love the parts of her that felt guilty.
She learned to hold space for the parts of her that felt angry.
She learned to soothe the parts of her that felt disappointed
And she learned to cherish the parts of her that were scattered everywhere else in pieces
And one by one the nurturer inside her, picked them all up,
Wrapped them in love and placed them back in her heart.

91

And in her freedom, she was reminded of the women who stay

In environments, relationships and circumstances that no longer serve them.

Their path of least resistance for now,

For children, for fright, for love,

May their hearts, spirits and thoughts be free to flee, if their bodies cannot.

Finding secret sanctuary, shelter, peace,

"Sisters, we stand with you and a thousand women surround you in love

This very minute, feel our collective strength.

We stand with you and in you."

92

The stars, the planets, the milky way - they stood still for her, that night

Time stopped just as she entered her sacred space,

She whispered, hand on heart and bowed her head.

Never in her entire life had she felt so complete.

Smudged, blessed, chosen and aligned,

Her healing exactly where it should be, with planetary forces at play.

She held space that night, with grace, poise, feminine elegance and strength,

Her path, her calling, her birthright confirmed,

She was home.

93

She knows that when the feminine has completed her return, there will be no secrets among women.

There will be no hiding - no holding back of information, no competition.

No edginess or awkward feelings of comparison.

It won't matter if their paths, teachings, words and beliefs are aligned or not,

For each woman will trust her own reason for being here so deeply,

She will stand so tall in her own beauty

that celebration and collaboration with her sisters will merge together as effortlessly as a kiss.

There was nothing more sexy to her than a man who knew himself,

A man who took responsibility for his own trauma, healing and salvation.

He didn't need her, he wanted her.

Capable, articulate, self soothing and full responsibility taken with intention to grow.

Sexy as hell, with eyes to match,

He saw straight through to her soul, shaking her core, matching her strength,

Loving her from the inside, sharing eyes just for her, conscious, awake and moving.

Painting pictures, writing intention, lyrics - deliberate creation.

Finding flow, harmonising, holding hands on unsteady walkways.

She'd fantasised about a man who knew what to do,

Who knew how to hold her, kiss her, stare at her while she slept.

She had no idea he was there all along, all she had to do was let go and fall.

95

She saw something in her that made her want to get to know her as a sister.

There was something about her that inspired her, that she recognised as some distant part of herself that she wanted to reignite

And she knew that she was in front of her right now for a reason beyond any girl crush, awe-like pedestal infatuation,

That she was in front of her right now so she could FEEL some of her divine energy

And in doing so, remember her own.

96

She was growing into a space of self healing,

A place where she connected to her higher priestess

And a deeper awareness of the whole of her was brewing.

A magical portal where souls entered the physical.

She began to understand, her most sacred and beautiful gift -

Her pathway to her rising began at her root,

That sacred place, where she allowed herself to be entered

Was now, through ritual and learning, understood to be holy.

Her divine gateway to wholeness not just a pathway to pleasure.

She became far more protective of her,

Way more intuitive about her.

She began speaking about her differently,

Touching her differently,

Allowing her to be touched differently.

She had shifted, still to fully digest her power

Yet feeling entirely different about her whole being.

Her yoni had woken her up.

97

She wore feathers in her hair,

A bindi on her third eye,

Cleansed her crystals in the moonlight

And howled to the moon.

She was a child of the sun.

The stars shone straight into her soul

And beams of light radiated to everyone who met her smile.

98

Rather than facing the storm, she ignored it and looked away.

Choosing her energy wisely, she danced with what-could-be instead -

She flirted with sunlight,

Entwined herself with pleasure

And gestured for joy to run wild within her,

For that was where inspiration lay.

Cool streams, bare feet on pebbles and moonlit shooting stars -

That's where the magic was and she knew it.

99

She was there for herself, that's all that mattered
In those moments of needing comfort and love and reassurance and touch,
For everything else was complicated where she was clear.
She knew what she needed, what she wanted and what her body craved
And she could give it to herself so very eloquently.
She spoke softly, whispered secrets, heard sources echo.
She was there for herself and that's all that mattered.

100

She was the elder, the grandmother, the great grandmother,

Loved, cherished and respected.

Beauty in age, graceful in nature, gentle in thought

And it was her final wish to slip away.

Her time to cross acknowledged -

A rite of passage,

A spirit preparing to rise.

Peace and stillness,

A granddaughters voice in the distance

Reading to her until she slept.

Whispers heard, far away stillness drifting closer,

Eyes closing, a century of heart beats slowing.

Strength and bravery in such vulnerability,

Unattached, ready and being received in light.

101

Kissing her fingertips in prayer as they glistened in the moonlit mountains of source -

She had come so far

Acknowledging her potential,

Recognising her source.

She blessed flow with feathers and crystals and sage,

A woman emerged where a girl once stood,

She felt wise, she felt seasoned, she felt bliss.

102

Big dreams were calling her to level up.

The need to be dissolved, challenged and stretched was undeniable,

Ready for a perspective so different, she knew it would blow everything that felt comfortable out of the water,

That comfort had swaddled her and done its job.

Now she had to stretch everything, now

Something bigger was calling.

With bravery, conviction, heart and love

She prepared her chrysalis.

103

And when fear bubbled up inside her and overtook her rationale, as it sometimes did,

She knew to find her balance

To bring herself back to centre,

That fear was just her human.

She knew better now than to give it control,

So she knelt on the ground beneath her,

Breathed fully and with love, she let her tears fall and wet the earth.

Connecting breath with the rise of her soul

She calmed herself back to centre,

So full of gratitude.

She heard her self in those moments

And trusted in her completely.

104

Drinking Cacao, smothering herself in coconut oil,
Seeking stillness and wearing feathers was her vibe now.

105

And when all chaos around her flew like demons and mad men, fire, anger and crashing waves,

She stood still grounded to the earth, connected to the sky -

Source flowing through her, channeling words, energy, wisdom.

A beacon of light, grounding energy, protective, nurturing, remaining still,

Solid in crisis, providing stability and safety.

Untold strength showering her with honour, for she was light,

She was love,

She was pure.

106

Feather earrings in honour of her soul sisters,
Bare feet in honour of Pachamama,
Incense in honour of her spirit,
Cacao in honour of source,
Tattoos in honour of her journey,
Meditation in honour of her Self.

107

She knew time alone,

It was her lover, her dreamy passion,

When she reflected herself and loved herself without boundaries.

And she also knew time with her sisters,

Time with other women; being heard,

Experiencing the raw openness of sharing, honesty and seeing each other.

An open channel of gratitude for what it takes to be a woman,

To know deep in your soul - of the courage, the fear, the trauma - the grit of another woman

Is healing beyond measure.

There is no pill to replace the sound of another's heart,

To be held in sacred space,

To be acknowledged, every word heard.

The soft soothing of sisters together, their love, their smiles, their hearts

In union with yours.

There is a place on this planet where women meet and gather and listen and speak

And is it called Sacred Circle.

It is where heartbeats are heard

And that's where she chose.

108

She wasn't late,
She wasn't early,
She was exactly right on time.

Through stillness and focus,
Balance and awareness,
She'd got her self to this point.

She was coming together with herself.
Little nudges, signs, the coming together of sisters, teachers, gifts -
Nothing went unnoticed.

Today she had just one job;
To revel in the wonder of it all, be the witness of her own uncovering,
Take a small hand in hers and laugh and play. She was right on time.

109

She served and she sang,

She channelled and she spoke,

She looked back and she looked forward,

Rewound time and stood in awe,

Felt excited and centred, still

Rising strong in delicate vulnerability,

Knowing she was about to go through the fire

Naked, her most powerful -

A volcano about to erupt

With her head to the stars and her feet taking steps.

One by one, she would walk in her own direction,

In her own light, her only shadow was hers and she embraced its presence.

Everything was clear,

Everything was reason,

The path was open.

110

Early morning, hand on heart, alone in the mist she whispered,

"Show me how I'm supported by the universe."

A voice said, "Trust. She wants the best for you. She has a plan."

Her voice flowed over her, like a cooling stream in flow.

No choice but to surrender and to do so in love

And sign after sign arrived, without fail; notes, timing, answers, movement.

Wind was twirling her around, child-like energy in the arms of her mother,

Smiling and laughing and breathing in play -

It was all there. Every direction was covered,

Completely supported, nothing serious happening here.

She breathed, relief washed over her,

She gave deep thanks to the wind and the rain and the earth and the stars.

111

When she was furious she felt so damn mad,
She could punch the sky, cry, kick and scream
And throw herself into pity with all her flaming energy -
And yet - she knew only to act when the flame had calmed.

That no woman had EVER found sanctity in the energy of rage,
That peace and manifesting and allowing of situations to unfold
Exactly as they were meant, happened in release,
So she released. She slept. She meditated. She drank cacao

And she listened to the inner voice and the voice of her sisters,
And she settled. She straightened. She aligned.
She remembered where her strength lay, she remembered she was on a growing edge.
Huge shifts were holding her with universal grace - all she had to do was be carried.
Surrender. Surrender. Surrender.

112

She'd been so deep in the mist, she'd forgotten there was clear blue sky,
She'd slipped unconsciously into a stream of hold ups and disconnect and fear and the kind of thinking that blurred her vision.
Drowning, she'd gone under, gasping for breath, panicking, unsafe, needing a light to be shone for her.
She knew this path, how deep she could sink, so she opened her eyes and moved.
She literally moved, got up, breathed fresh air, soothed herself that very second with nourishment
And was reminded of her name, that her life was sacred,
That there was a calling on her life that was bigger than this.
She remembered, she released, grip loosened, smile ignited, eyes closed in gratitude.
Her knowing flowed into her, she knew what to do and how to do it,
She saw herself once more, she was here to grow and she was moving.

113

She stared into the roaring fire

So close, her breath consumed by its power.

With closed eyes, hands at prayer

She whispered soft words of intent deep into the night.

The world so still, just cracks and licks from jumping flames.

In the presence of sacred sisterhood

Women gathered in silent respect,

Prayers being answered,

Souls blessed,

Hearts healed,

Old messages burning to cinders,

Dreams being birthed.

Like midwives for each other, they gathered in prayer.

Oh that drum,

Bringing awareness back,

Giving thanks for the element of purification.

One by one whispers of a song turned to the collective rise of the feminine,

As their voices rose and each woman chanted and breathed and harmonised with her sister.

Deep breaths taken, hands on hearts, drums beating, rising to their feet

They circled and stomped and laughed and drummed and shook and hollered!

Like the Shamans and witches and manifestors of the past,

They held true power.

THIS is celebration, THIS is sisterhood, THIS is the calling of spirits, of ancestors and healing.

THIS is how to love your sisters, THIS is how to rise together.

114

In the midst of confusion, with nothing more than an image in her mind,
He arrived. Standing right in front of her to sweep her off her feet.
No choice, just flow, the only way to go.
The universe at play, knowing her path hadn't even begun.

And when she took his hand, his heart, his breath,
She had no idea of the journey, the destination or the gravitas of her conviction.
Would he lead her or would she lead him?
Neither of them knew, they only recognised that their footsteps and their hands were entwined.

And so they follow, they lead, they swerve, they curve around each other,
Dancing in connection one moment, then deep in a personal journey the next,
Unravelling past lives, blending life assignments, core visions, deeply held musts.
She held his hand, taking him close to her face, she loved him and he loved her.

115

If she remembers herself
At her core,
Who she is,
What she needs,
Her visions and her greatest dreams,
Then she has unlimited power.

116

And in those moments when she was by herself
Naked, with her thoughts, no one watching,
She closed her eyes and listened.
The beat of her heart,
Her rhythmical breath,
The sound of her Self.
When no-one was watching
She melted all resistance away,
Nothing to say,
Nothing to think,
Open space to free her spirit -
An honouring of her Self.
Sanctuary found,
Her heart a resting place,
She remembered everything.

117

She did it just for her -

For no other reason, that it resonated.

She felt called,

Compelled,

Every single part of her said YES.

So she took herself off

And sat and listened and shared,

And opened and deepened and forgave and sang a song of love,

Realising in that moment exactly what she came for.

For it arrived in her heart as a gift,

She was ready to return.

118

Stillness of morning,

Birdsong,

Cool air.

Basking in the promise of a day filled with love,

She meditated.

She listened

And she felt her heart expand.

119

Her Self was crying.

While her human could be sidelined,

Her Self screamed for connection.

She craved freedom,

To live and to be,

To walk barefoot,

Feel the sun on her face,

Watch the sunset

And feel sand squeeze between her toes.

Her soul needed some love,

So she gave her the moon as a gift.

120

And the crone inside spoke to her

Like an older sister, she asked questions,

Peeled back layers of maiden habits to reveal wiser words,

Uncovered the truth,

Laid bare an old wound to be healed.

And there she was,

Seeing the truth,

Acting from deeper ancient wisdom.

A pattern broken this time,

She melted back into the arms of her wiser self,

Smiling, trusting and knowing herself more than ever before -

Oh so grateful for her years, her mistakes and the elder in her,

She loved her dearly.

121

When she drummed, her ancestors heard.
When she called them in, her spirits rose.
A call for gathering -
The message of the drum travelled so far.
Energy rising,
Trusting their graceful presence,
Medicine for her highest good.
Healing: herself, her sisters, every woman.
Rhythm deepening their collective journey,
Distant footsteps gathering, rising, moving.
She was woman medicine.

122

When she closed her eyes she was by her self,

With her Self,

For her Self.

And when she meandered into that place

And stayed there long enough

Her thoughts of worry and questions and not knowing

Took her on a river which flowed straight into love.

Strong appreciation for her body, her space, her own inner world

Where no-one was allowed.

Her secrets kept safe, her wonders and dreams held her

And sparkled and lit her beauty.

She did not need to know anything right now,

She only needed to embrace the luxury of her Self.

123

She reflected with every single star dusted cell
How truly wonderful it was to be bathed in light,
How far she'd come,
And how far she was willing to go.

124

She was coming,

Coming to get her true self.

On her way -

Smiling, courting her,

Playing with her,

Luring her with love and fun and fire and messages.

Sign posts everywhere of where to find her,

Navigating her way,

The spirits calling her home

To where she belonged,

To what she was meant to be doing.

No more dancing on the edges,

But being put right in the ring of fire.

Right in the middle,

To rise up and shine and be exactly who she was being called to be.

125

She was made of rivers and lakes,
sand dunes and hills,
shooting stars and wishes,
hidden caves and unseen jewels.

She was made of temples and waterfalls,
earth and clay,
roots right down to her soul
and a thousand suns that lit her path.

126

She needed no-one else's permission
To bless herself,
To smudge her field,
To honour her wisdom,
To feel the deepest rivers that ran through the most private crevices of her mind.

She needed no-one else's permission
To regard herself as sacred,
To breathe into her own beauty,
To run wild with her own soul,
To discover her own alignment, her inner priestess, her most intimate sacred temple.

127

She stared at herself so deeply she was a stranger.

She looked deep into her own eyes seeking the soul within,

She found truth and stillness, stars and crystals.

Moons and tsunamis shook through her as

Scars disappeared, trauma disintegrated like sand running through open fingers.

Trembling, she was unearthing an angel.

Stumbling straight into the wise queen.

An awakening woman was staring back.

128

She had chosen to disengage, to walk alone and find herself -
A journey just for her,
Layers had been exposed revealing cuts and traumas,
Weaknesses and pain
And one by one, she had soothed and kissed
And stroked them away.
Ceremony and ritual, plants and dance.

129

And just to lay on the earth

And appreciate everything about herself and this time,

This space and this moment.

Everything has purpose,

The dark and the light.

She had travelled so far

And now was time to lay still

And soak up her essence,

To bless her Self

With love, with contentment and pure light.

130

She was pure,
She was strong,
She decided to fight,
She made it clear -
She wasn't going away.

131

Every single day
She got up,
She kept going,
Tried not to look back.
Her future was her only project.

132

And guilt - she realised - hung like a shackle around her neck;

Heavy, dark and lonely,

She felt it all the time.

The weight of it sank to the pit of her stomach

And it dawned on her,

If she wanted to run as fast as she said she did

She would have to lighten the load.

She would have no choice but to let it go,

She couldn't carry it around with her anymore.

To be truly free, she would have to unshackle her Self

And no-one could do it for her.

133

"Find your centre", she whispered into the dark.

She was the only one to hear, her whisper was so faint.

She held out an arm to steady her.

Deep in the medicine, breathing in the fresh cool night straight out of the thick field of Madre.

She wobbled, and heard her again. "Find your centre."

She straightened.

They both did,

Because in the asking of her to find her centre, she found hers too.

And together they walked in silence, only their breath to be heard, close by each other.

Medicine sisters walking along the path, silence except for the distant drumming from the yurt.

She will never forget that night. The stillness they both felt, the composure, such meaningful words spoken through her, for them both.

134

And she sat in stillness,
Open to hearing whispers from above, below, behind and in front.
Smiling guides and mentors flocked to her side,
So pleased to have been acknowledged.
Unseen wisdom just a breath away -
She was never alone.

FIRE CEREMONY CHANT

Fire, fire, fire,

Whisper my desire.

In your arms, you hold my prayers,

Oh fire, fire, fire.

(Created on A Woman's Blessing retreat)

HER PRAYER

I am balanced.

I am light.

I am calm.

I am beautiful.

I am joy.

I am loving.

I ground myself.

My power is strong, innate, inbuilt.

I am calm and in balance, I shine in my own light.

CACAO PRAYER

To the elders, the wise ones, the ones who knew;
To the ancestors, the men and women who sought refuge and holy communion with Cacao,
To the ones who believed, who trusted and who called in the spirits -
We honour you.

To the Mayans;
To the ancient tribes and communities,
To the ones who kept the spirit of Cacao alive and close to their hearts for centuries -
We thank you.

To the spirit of Cacao,
For your wisdom, your nutrients;
To your heart warming nourishment,
We bow to you.

To the ones who serve cacao today,
Who encourage connection with this ancient knowledge and wisdom;
To the ones who blend old worlds with new -
Please continue.

To the ones who are drinking Cacao around the world this very moment;
To the women who found their voice, their power, their might
And the women who are struggling, lost and hidden -
We drink for you.
A'ho

SMUDGING PRAYER

With this smoke I call in our protective spirits, ancestors and angels.

May healing positive energy surround our sacred circle,

May this smoke purify, cleanse and release all energy which no longer serves us.

A temple of light will safely guide us,

To bring deep peace, wholeness and love.

A'ho

HER PRAYER TO THE GUIDES

With this candle, I call you.

With this candle, I ask for your guidance.

With this candle, I am open.

With this candle, I am ready to hear your whispers.

With this candle, I feel you with me.

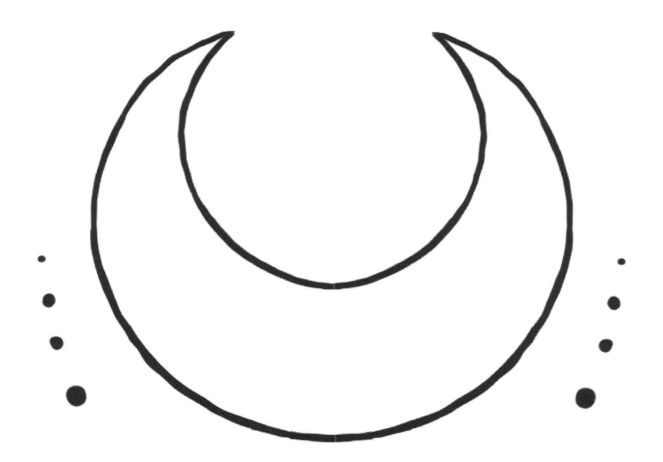

A CLOSING BLESSING

As we take great care to close this sacred space,
We bring our awareness to the spirits who surrounded us in our blessed circle.
For the ancestors who safely delivered us here to this very moment,
For the wisdom of angels and divine femininity,
For our healing, strength and inner power.
To the masters, the priestesses, the gate keepers and secret holders -
We appreciate your guidance and love in this beautiful ceremony.
A'ho

SPIRIT GUIDES

Close your eyes and open a page where you feel intuitively.
Read about your chosen Spirit Guide and hold her close today.

SKY LARK

Sky Lark is loving and nurturing, yet pragmatic and practical. She feels deeply, accepts her sensitivity and uses ritual, affirmation & healthy new habits to restore herself. She is open, loves her sisters like blood and oozes beauty and love.

This Spirit Guide has been chosen by you for a reason. Take time today to nurture yourself, take her loving spirit and cloak yourself with self love. Do something that makes you smile, that makes you feel special; something that fills you up with love.

Sky Lark also has a pragmatic and practical element to her and in choosing her, feel free to let the practical side of you shine today. Maybe there's something you've been avoiding, something you really need to get done. Today is a good day to hold her spirit with you as you delve into those things you've been putting off, jobs to do, crossing off items on a list, making a list and organising one thing that will make your life easier.

She is deeply sensitive, so ensure that you plug into your sensitivity today. By nurturing yourself and fuelling yourself with some love you could well plug straight into your sensitive soul, giving her some nourishment and attention. She's there always and maybe today is the day she needs your attention and focus.

Help her by using a ritual to soothe any worries she has or give her problem/s to the universe to lift off her shoulders.

A simple ritual would be to find something from nature - a stone, a leaf, a feather, a flower.

- Find an item that resonates with you.
- Find somewhere quiet to sit; light a candle, breathe deeply and make yourself comfortable.
- Hold your item to your heart. Whisper your concern/s you have no answers for yet into your hand and onto your item.
- Next, place it next to your candle and say:

"Sky Lark, I give this to you and the Universe to hold for me. Please whisper your guidance and help me to hear your thoughts. I release this to you and trust that guidance will come in the form of inspired ideas, interesting coincidences and people who make me smile."

Smile, give your thanks and blow out the candle when you are ready.

CLEAR SPIRIT

Clear Spirit is strong and clear, securing her guidance from the universe. She is sure footed – only acting when she feels moved to, she trusts that things will work out. She is mindful, a truth teller, sees the playfulness of life, encouraging others to do the same.

This beautiful angel is giggling right next to you. "Nothing serious happening here", she smiles as she strokes your face and kisses your brow.

Close your eyes and feel her playfulness dancing around you. Childlike energy, she beats her drum for you, celebrating every cell in your body; thanking the universe for your presence in this time and settling to sit opposite to you in prayer.

You are being called today to be brave, to act from inspiration only, to put yourself where is comfortable. Hold yourself in vibrational alignment - meaning; do what resonates today: do what fills you up, inspires you or makes you tingle with enthusiasm.

For the world will still turn, plates will still spin, conversations are still being had by people about you, for your greatest benefit.

All is well.

Settle yourself with this ritual and bring her in to guide you.

- Sit comfortably.
- Close your eyes.
- Feel her playful spirit and breathe with her rhythm.
- In… out… in… out... in time with her breath; slowing each breath, feeling heavier in your body as your shoulders relax and you connect with your ground.
- Repeat:

"I am listening for divine direction. I have help. I will act when I am called and I will know when I receive a message from pure, source energy. I trust. All is well."

RISING ROCK

Rising Rock is a fierce mama. She offers protection, guidance and wisdom. She uses deep knowing and lifetimes of experiences to build foundations of strength on which she walks, encouraging others to do the same. She is kind, tactile, inexplicably beautiful, protects her boundaries and walks with love.

your hands chose Rising Rock today, it's because you are being offered her protection. You are being invited protect your space, to honour your boundaries - just as she does - and to do so with love, kindness and tact.

here is no need to rush straight in, instead think about what you really need and what you really want.

hen ask yourself, quietly on your own:

"If I needed to protect a boundary today, which one would I protect?"

Where do you need to say no? Where are you feeling taken advantage of, not listened to or ignored? Start here.

se Rising Rock and this ritual to claim your space and word your boundary protection clearly and in love.

- Find somewhere quiet.
- Light a candle and breath for a few minutes to calm and centre yourself.
- Place your right hand over your heart, the left side of your chest.
- Ask yourself "What 3 things do I need to say in this situation?"
- Write down clear, short sentences - the 3 things you need the other person to know in order that you claim your boundary.
- When you have finished ask Rising Rock for her protection, guidance and wisdom.

he will offer you the ideal time to deliver your 3 things, and you will do so in a calm way; with clear guidance, ith love and with grace. She is a fierce mama who will be with you. You are not alone, you have divine essings in this situation.

FOREST HEART

She embraces feminine softness, vulnerability and authenticity. With it she is strong, articulate, self-aware and in tune with her body's needs. A natural nurturer, aware of the feelings and needs of others, she inspires and cheer leads from the sidelines for every human she loves.

The message for you here on this page is to embrace your femininity, vulnerability and authenticity.

So often misunderstood for being weak or soft, Forest Heart would like to offer you another perspective. She embraces her feminine energy and vulnerability with incredible strength, she is so articulate and she takes time to tune into her own body's needs. She is inviting you to do the same today.

What is your body saying today? Is there a part of your body that is aching, calling, whispering a message to you?

It might be time to rest, to take yourself off somewhere private and just BE with your body. You may be being called today to delve into the depths of your femininity, your needs, your desires.

You might have let your attention to the goddess in you slide, you may be being called to go deeper into your sexual desires, self pleasure, comfort or honouring. To take yourself into your own pleasure sexually is powerful, yet you honour the softness in you. Your honouring comes from a place of authenticity when you are alone and by yourself.

What does your body need? Where do you need to place your attention, focus, healing hands or lightest touch?

Take some time with this ritual:

- Find yourself a space which is quiet and undisturbed.
- Light a candle, lie down and place your hands on your body.
- Breathe. Move your hands where they are needed, where they are desired to go.
- Slow, even breath in. Slow, even breath out.
- Take your attention from your headspace down into your heart space, your womb space, your base chakra.
- Listen and respond as you are called.

OCEAN COOL

**Grace, beauty, power and dignity describes Ocean Cool perfectly.
A queen of ceremony, ritual and intention; she is deliberate in her thought, wise beyond her years, fun, a deep thinker and researcher with a feminine strength that matches the power of her presence.**

If you chose Ocean Cool today you can trust that she guided you to this page. She is asking something of you. She is asking you to be as deliberate about your thoughts today as she is every day.

This queen of ceremony has thought and intention running through her body; like energetic highways they are strong and clear and free flowing. You are being called to step up today. To consider your own energetic highways, to keep them open - which means to keep the flow of good and positive energy moving. That means being deliberate in your thoughts, for your thoughts are the vehicles on your energetic highway.

Sense into the quality of your thoughts. Are your thoughts negative, worried, fearful or anxiety fuelled? Are you literally creating traffic in your mind with your thoughts or are you calm, happy, free flowing, going with the flow, feeling the energy move smoothly through you?

Intentional thought mixed with free flowing fun is where you create everything you ever wanted. Not overthinking, just being attentive to your desires. Recognising when you would love a manifestation to come to fruition and then going about your day; enjoying your world, singing to songs on the radio, laughing and remembering the funniest of times.

Ocean Cool is fun. She enjoys everything - the sip of her Cacao, the lighting of her candles, the ritual of placing rocks where she intuitively feels they should be to indicate to the universe her deepest most playful wishes... an intentional kiss placed on a lovers lips. She. Enjoys. Everything.

Take some time to be with Ocean Cool today. She is asking 4 things of you:

- Sit in presence with yourself, enjoy feeling yourself breathe without effort while listening to the birds, music or pure silence.
- Change your plans today so they incorporate something really fun, something that's going to make you smile from ear to ear - stopping off for a flat white, taking a detour to a beach, driving the country way to your destination.
- Ask the universe for time with an animal. A cat, dog, horse, rabbit, an animal that you can sit with comfortably who will want your playful attention and focus.
- And finally walk barefoot on the grass, the earth, the sand… let pachamama know you feel her and let her remind you - she is your support, your ground and your very being.

QUIET RIVER

She's quiet and reserved, thoughtful and contemplative. Careful with her actions, she takes time with her decisions, seeks out her own self development and loves conversations steeped in depth, meaning and sincerity. Her smile is infectious, her loyalty and dedication admirable.

She sees you. That's why you found her on this page. She sees your smile, your loyalty and your dedication to yourself, because you always come back to you.

She is asking today that you come back to your inner sanctuary; that are you are little quiet today - but you find time for solitude, that you speak a little less today, listen more, meditate a little and that the conversations you have focus on the meaningful and deep.

When you surround yourself with people, when conversations are fast and flowing and opinions are flying it's easy to get lost in the party, squash feelings to the seat of your stomach to be dealt with later - today you might find is your metaphorical 'later'.

Is there something you've been meaning to read?

Is there a conversation about something truly meaningful you've been meaning to have with a loved one or friend?

Is there a question on your mind that you have been meaning to research and understand on a deeper level?

Today is the day to do it.

You're not on your own - Quiet River is next to you. Like a soothing, comforting, babbling brooke. Just right here, helping you flow to the right information; helping your conversations flow, your words will come, deeper understandings to be felt. You will tune into yourself and another with ease.

Smile with yourself today, enjoy the quiet, make space for the thoughtful.

Energy is perfectly aligned for you. You are free.

WILD WIND

Wild Wind is playful and strong, loving and articulate. An inquiring mind, she's an explorer craving adventure and fun, pleasing. She pleases herself and has no time for limitation, rules or other peoples opinion. She values a deep connection to herself and a few chosen ones, seeing friends as family. Wild Wind loves time on her own, knows what she needs and is bold in the asking of it.

Wild Wind's message to you is to find your playful, put yourself first and please yourself today.

She is sending you a clear message - "Find the child in you, have fun and don't give a care as to what other people think."

She is fun and is beckoning the fun in you to emerge, to laugh at the ridiculous and find teeny moments to be appreciative of.

Wild Wind can be a whirlwind! She'll dress how she pleases with absolutely no regard to what another thinks; she will love her wild hair, she has no time for another's opinion on her. She approves of herself entirely and focuses on one thing only - pleasing herself. In fact, she revels in it!

Find the Wild Wind in you. Feel her giggling in front of you, like a small child with wild hair, jumping up and down for your attention.

Go with her, find your wild today.

Open your wardrobe and dress up for YOU.

Make something to eat that is ENTIRELY soul filling, eat it with your fingers and lick the plate.

Dance to loud music and feel your 3rd eye open.

And when all that is done, enjoy your own space. Ask for your privacy, soothe yourself, be bold in the asking of it, close your eyes and watch the sparkles in your energy field gently float to the floor as you smile your way through your peace and inner contentment. For Wild Wind calms also; she values herself deeply and will plug in to her source, sit with her crystals and refuel.

She is your greatest teacher. Be open to her, she is in you.

A TRIBUTE TO HER

A blonde bombshell, you could say.

Tall, beautiful, striking, slender and completely, unequivocally kick-ass - that was clear.

She walked in with style for sure; with grace, humility, SUCH a smile. I loved her instantly.

So so brave. For two nights, Mother Ayahuasca held her -

Whispered messages, showed her what she never wanted to see,

But what she needed to see, to see her to the end.

Weak, ready to give up, tired. So, so tired, ready to go,

No more fight, just tears and exhaustion and yes, fear.

But with love and rest and talking and hugs she remembered who she was

And she left ready. Ready to fight if she needed to; with will to live,

Determination to breathe and to plan and to imagine and to see a future.

And that's how she did it - right to the end - with will, with fight, with no-nonsense, kick ass, outspoken, say-it-as

it-is force.

So brave. So, so brave and then ready. Resigned, quieter I love you's.

She slipped away, last breath whispered; to no pain, to kick ass from the other side,

To be heard a different way,

To connect more clearly than ever before.

To be tough, to encourage, to remind

All women: you can do this, you've GOT this, you have. You really, really have.

ABOUT THE AUTHOR

A small girl in a family with her Mum, Dad and her brother. She loved to write. She studied, read her books, sought good grades and followed the rules. Walking through the steps of life; she travelled, she danced, she followed her intuition within the lines: a job, a career, book deals, media coverage, TV, engaged and married. And then her bubble burst. The unexpected death of her Daddy, stunned that her marriage was no longer for her and an urge to test herself so strong that it guided her to leave behind a life and see what she could do - she opened her wings wide and flew off the edge of her world.

Universal laws introduced themselves to her. Love: a man arrived, a teenage daughter, a brand new baby and a twist. For in her flying and breathing new life, she flouted more rules, cut the ties of safety and clinging on for dear life - she dove head first into an unknown world. Shamanism, plant medicine, long nights, deep hurt spilling over, rest so deep she thought she would never return, drumming into the darkness, releasing a voice. A message not just heard but gifted deep into another's soul. Peeling off layers of expectation to reveal a connection to source, feeling messages, being guided, learning to trust and learning that normal was not as she had been sold.

Taking the hand of her future self, she drank, she meditated and held her space, sang and drummed. She deepened and grew into her wisdom to enable other women to find theirs. She serves, she channels, holds space to bring women together and sit in sacred circle. She heals, she expands, she manifests and words tumble onto a page: to heal old wounds, hers and those of her sisters of the world.

The emergence of an ancient soul, a medicine woman, bringing forth HER medicine for the empowering of the rising feminine, encouraging the voices of millions of women. She comforts and soothes, her voice calm but clear and direct.

She draws sustenance, power and remembering from her mountain - where her personal pilgrimage began - she places herself there for guidance and reassurance. Madre draws her back from time to time, paying her unexpected visits to remind her she is with her and in her. The sacred Cacao she lovingly prepares nourishes her into a soothing mind, where she can do her work. For she knows that this life is a quest to connect her to her higher self and serve the feminine purposefully while she is here; a nurturer, a mother, a teacher, a guide, a friend, a lover. She holds her Self and you sweet sister, so so dear to her heart.

PRAISE

"What an amazing en envelope of expression, much needed and appreciated in this wave of repetitive sameness. It's like petals thrown on to the waters of a still lake, to be carried away by its depth. Beautiful expressions of a revival into the simple and profound. Super too, all this divinity"
Pitt Ewart, Shaman

"Absolutely stunning, beautiful! Every woman, everywhere, will feel these words deep in her soul...it's a brilliant piece of writing"
Sarah Ward. Womens healer & Red Tent facilitator

"I was going to read bits here and there but once I started, I couldn't put it down. I kept telling myself when I get to something that doesn't pull me in, I will stop. I didn't get to that point. Everything spoke to me about something in my life. Quite a few of the poems resonated with me so strongly I wondered if she had been reading my thoughts. I let fate choose a Spirit Guide for me and it was Quiet River. I feel like she will help me with my journey to my Queening ceremony"
Sylvie Hirst, Independent Celebrant

"An instinctive journey of remembrance for women everywhere"
Maria Fotiou, Shamanic Healer & Intuitive Guide

"Lynette's deep connection to Spirit and her passion for empowering women is beautifully evident in this powerful book. Perfect for individual or group use, these wise and graceful words truly are a blessed resource"
Reverend Deb Connor, Author of 'The Little Book of Dao', Spirit Guided Artist, Interfaith Minister and Daoist Priest

---

"Lynette's words are beautiful and her spirit pours from her soul onto the pages of this book. It's a divine representation of what it means to be sacred"
Rev Lisa Dooley RMT/Spiritual Business Mentor, Channelled Inspirations

---

"This beautiful poetry conveys a woman's lifetime journey - all the flavours and seasons of the feminine - and how a circle of brave sisters can hold her through that process. Recommended for deep reflection and affirmation of womanhood"
Tessa Venuti Sanderson, Red Tent facilitator Author of 'Ruby Luna's Curious Journey'

"This book took my spirit on a ride of all aspects of the amazing feminine journey. Loved the rawness, honesty and loving vibes from the author and her magical connection"
Natalie Oakley, Empathic Human Conduit

I feel this book as poetry that kindles your fire, so that you remember to maintain it. It is an intuitive tool that can guide you almost like a tarot. Born from ashes and transformation. You can feel the love and care of Lynette and the comfort she brings through her beautiful feminine nature. I bless the woman she is, and the beautiful space she holds for others"
Paula Maria. Shamama

'A beautiful written and poetic book that honours recognising your innate strength, personal feminine power and the divine in you. An easy read, full of shamaic magick that you can drink in slowly and with ease"
Rachael Claire, Shaman

"I couldn't stop crying from the beginning to the end. So many moments of my life seem to be written and explained by her words. This could be the push I need to seek myself and give myself the power to BE myself. I am not alone"
Virginia Gonzalez Pinto, Earth Mother

LOVE LETTERS

If these words have found your heart, made an imprint on your soul and resonated with your being, I would love to know.

Please message me:

lynette@awomansblessing.com

SISTERHOOD

Join Lynette in sacred circle at one of her events:

Find out more on: www.awomansblessing.com

For more rituals to download visit our shop: www.awomansblessing.com/shop

Join our ever expanding community: www.facebook.com/awomansblessing

Join our Strength Sister Community group: www.facebook.com/groups/strengthsistercommunity

Connect with our visual sisterhood: www.instagram.com/awomansblessing
and www.instagram.com/thelynetteallen for a personal connection with Lynette

Connect to our beautiful illustrator on www.instagram.com/ami_suel/

Printed in Great Britain
by Amazon